Growing
Schools?

Anna Shaw
School Ministry Development Officer

GROVE BOOKS LIMITED
RIDLEY HALL RD CAMBRIDGE CB3 9HU

Contents

Dedication

This book is dedicated to my husband, the Revd Graham Shaw, and children Barney, Daniel and Ruth. Their insights and experiences both challenge and encourage me.

Acknowledgments

I am grateful for the support of many critical friends whose comments on drafts have improved the text enormously, and to Howard Worsley for his thoughtful supervision.

First Impression January 2025
ISSN 2041-0964
ISBN 978 1 78827 441 8

1 Introduction

I well remember my sense of excitement, pride and daunted responsibility as I took on my first class in 2004. I had become a Christian six years previously and now I longed to understand what it meant to be a *Christian* teacher. What difference could, or should, my worldview make? Instinctively, it felt like an abuse of power that I should in any way proselytize my pupils, and yet I longed for everyone around me to know Jesus. How should I hold myself as a Christian teacher, both wanting to share my faith but also wanting to respect the power imbalance in the classroom context?

'Growing Faith' is a phrase used within the Church of England to represent a desire for culture shift so that children and families are at the heart of its ministry and mission facilitated by schools, households and churches collaborating better. But this raises many questions around the place of *Growing Faith* within a school system which needs to be open and inclusive to children of all backgrounds.

For me, the answer took shape more clearly a couple of years later. My immediate team of colleagues did not share my faith, but were curious about how I was going to mark Lent. At the time, our school was a challenging place to work due to issues of workplace harassment and bullying. I had read in Phil 2.14 that I should do everything 'without complaining and arguing.' This was certainly not how I was living. So, I answered that I would be giving up 'complaining and arguing' for Lent. They decided to join in. What unfolded was extraordinary. As other staff across the school grew more embittered and depressed, the mood within our teaching team lightened. The difference became increasingly marked. So much so that, at the end of term, one colleague pronounced, 'This Lent has taught me so much. Whilst I am not about to become a Christian, *I can see that living God's way works!'*

Wow! Here I had some form of an answer. What did it mean to be a Christian teacher? To take God's word seriously and live it out in such a way that others around, be they pupils or adults, had the chance to see that 'living God's way works'? My colleagues were free to join in to the degree with which they felt comfortable. There was no compulsion that they should become Christians, but they had enjoyed the opportunity to participate and to draw nearer to God. Now they started to ask questions and to seek deeper understanding. I had their invitation to give them a reason for the hope that I had (1 Pet 3.15).

2 Distinctively/Deeply Christian

Having found an answer to the personal question, a parallel global question remained: what difference could, or should, it make that [at that time] church schools were required by SIAMS to be 'distinctively Christian'?

This question has long been debated. Reputedly, Lord Runcie, the former Archbishop of Canterbury, reflected that church schools gave the church opportunity to:

> Nourish those of the faith;
> encourage those of other faiths;
> challenge those who have no faith.[1]

More recently, the *Church of England Vision for Education: Deeply Christian, Serving the Common Good* report (which underpins the current SIAMS framework, which in turn influences individual school praxis) states a vision for education where pupils 'leave school with a rich experience and understanding of Christianity' and where there is a commitment 'to offering them an encounter with Jesus Christ and the Christian faith and practice in a way that enhances their lives.'[2]

For some over the years this discourse has been uncomfortable. With its roots in a very confessional approach to education in Victorian times, church schools have sometimes been treated by government and secularists with mistrust. Perhaps this was why the language of 'distinctively Christian' was dropped a decade ago in favour of 'deeply Christian' because this was felt to be more inclusive. Whilst it is excellent to seek to include, this linguist shift has cut short some of the wrestling with what distinctively Christian might mean. Most would agree that no education is truly neutral of worldview.[3] Possibly a strength of church schools is that they are transparent about their underpinning values and worldview, giving freedom to all in how they wish to interact with this.

Continuing the story from earlier, a new head teacher arrived at my school, who had taken time out to research how children develop spiritually. He had developed his Collective Worship approach around this and it was radically different from anything I had hitherto encountered. Adults and children all engaged together throughout the week. On Mondays there was a magazine-style Collective Worship format (much like *Blue Peter* with its weekly craft, pictures wall, presenter challenge, visitor slot etc). There would be a linked musical introduction (often from the charts), a Bible story / extract, a literature extract that picked up the theme, recurring characters who would dramatize something of the teaching point, a pupil messy challenge etc. It was very eclectic. Tuesdays was visitor Collective Worship, reflecting on the same theme, delivered by a local church member or by a Christian member of staff. Pupils were then left to join the dots during their class Thoughtful Times on Wednesdays, when they were given a leaflet with quotations, proverbs and stories, some questions and space to discuss the week's theme and opportunity to prepare a response to share in Friday's Collective Worship or to write in their personal reflective journals. There was a lot of opportunity in the new set-up for pupils to ask their own questions, to have significant space for their own reflection and to be able to lead others. It was less prescriptive, less didactic, more child-led.

My pupils loved the change. In particular, one girl came with unending questions and would arrive back from playtimes spent in the outdoor prayer space curious about what she felt God was teaching her. She was not from a household where religious faith was practised and saw things with fresh eyes. However, as her class teacher, I was limited in the extent to which I could support her. I was cautious about the power dynamics of my being her teacher. An additional challenge was that she was soon to move on to the community secondary school. Her family, who were open to her questions, had no idea how to engage with her ponderings or how to help her develop spiritually. We needed the local church.

She wanted to go, and her family were happy to let her. But sadly, the local Church of England church was not able to welcome and support her. Suddenly it dawned on me that the spiritual development which the school was offering was a poorer version without the church being deeply present with us.

The local Christian community, experienced through local churches of all denominations, had potential to fill the areas in which we were lacking as a church school community. In the end, support for her came from Christians from another denomination who came into school to run a Bible club and then invited her to join them at their youth club and Sunday gathering. This approach might be called kingdom witness rather than denominational witness (in this case Church of England) because of its engagement with the wider Christian community.

In the same way, although aspects of this book pertain to church schools, much also applies in community schools. Community schools can engage with the

Growing Faith culture shift, though it certainly requires more wisdom and prayer to know how best to proceed.

Church schools do a remarkable job in living out a form of Christian community and giving access to the teaching and person of Jesus. But even in my superb local church school, where the Bible is taught clearly and where deep and authentic Christian community is offered, there are limitations that cannot be met without the involvement of the local church(es). The head teacher openly acknowledges this and actively seeks partnership. However, although schools have huge potential to empower spiritual development, they are often limited by some, or many, of these factors:

- lack of clarity amongst senior church school leaders and governors regarding what it means to be deeply Christian;
- a shortage of Christian staff members to help embed Christian community and offer encounter with the person and teaching of Jesus;
- increasing pressure from secular parents;
- aging and diminishing local church congregation(s);
- increasing pressure on head teachers and clergy, leaving them too time-poor to invest strategically or even have time for personal relationship;
- church services that are inaccessible to children or families who are seeking to explore;
- difficulty in finding effective Christian governors;
- churches in vacancy, awaiting the appointment of a new incumbent or subject to a pastoral re-organization scheme.

In 2019, a report entitled *Growing Faith: Churches, Schools and Households (GS2121)* was taken to General Synod.[4] In it, the authors noted that there have been regular reports for over 35 years on the spiritual development of children and young people from both education as well as church mission and ministry perspectives. Yet somehow, despite repeated calls for more integrated working of church and school and a focus on putting the young person at the centre, there had been little impact.

But the winds of change are blowing.

Following this *Growing Faith* report and the struggles of the pandemic, we find ourselves in a new season, with new opportunities. The purpose of this booklet is to help readers understand the changes afoot and to offer support for engaging wisely, alert to both the possibilities and the challenges.

To give a flavour of this culture change, *kairos* moment and to demonstrate that it cuts across the Church of England at many levels, here are a few examples of places where actions, priorities and culture are shifting across the institution:

- The *Growing Faith Foundation* has come into being. It is not an activity or a programme but rather it is led as 'a movement that exists to put children, young people and families instinctively at the heart of the mission and ministry of the Church of England, by bringing about a change in culture and practice. It involves *churches, schools* and *households* working together to help children, young people and families have life in all its fullness.'[5]
- The Church of England Education Office has launched the *FLOURISH* network with the goal of seeing 450 worshipping communities pioneered in schools and colleges by 2030, so that Christian discipleship is made accessible to those pupils and families who are interested.[6] There is significant funding being made available, with pilots starting in the first 40 locations in September 2024.
- *'Doubling the number of children and young active disciples in the Church of England by 2030'* is the first stated bold outcome of the current National Church of England Vision and Strategy team.
- The above is giving rise to many initiatives on many fronts, with finances prioritized for them. This includes the recruitment of *3000 new, paid children's and youth workers and 27,000 children and youth volunteers*, many of whom will seek to link church and school more holistically and who will be looking to support households more deeply.
- As a sign of the change in culture, the *Archbishops' Council* now requires that papers presented to them must indicate explicitly how they support the six bold outcomes of their vision and strategy (top of which is the growing younger goal above).

Although this book is written in the context of the current *Growing Faith, kairos* moment, it is intended as a text that can support thinking well into the future. The reflections and questions that follow have been written in the hope of supporting schools, churches and households to partner more effectively indefinitely.

3 Growing Faith

In 2019 Andy Wolfe, Executive Director of Education for the Church of England, wrote a helpful summary for schools, reflecting on the General Synod *Growing Faith* paper.[7] In it, he pointed out that although households, schools and churches can each be places where children and young people can be supported and developed spiritually, the most powerful opportunities for spiritual development occur where those three institutions are able to work together, which he expressed like this:

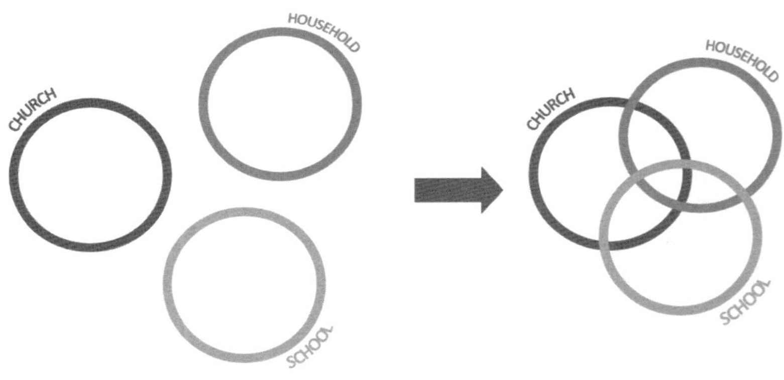

This should not surprise us. The biblical model for the spiritual development of children and young people is through the family, with them enjoying the support of the wider community. Parents are instructed intentionally to train their children in righteousness (Prov 22.6), and to be proactive in using all moments of life for this (Deut 6.4–9)—not just when gathered together at formal moments of religious observance. In biblical times 'family' was a much broader grouping than we see in the nuclear families of Western Europe today. Instead, multiple generations lived together under one roof with servants also included in the mix. Although the task of spiritually developing the next generation sat primarily with parents, it was actively supported by this wider family and then further upheld by the whole community. Through major festivals like Passover and Purim, through regular local gatherings and through the weekly rhythm of *shabbat*, together they retold the stories of their faith.

As Lucy Moore, head of the *Growing Faith Foundation*, has observed, these influences come together in the narrative in Luke 2 in which twelve-year-old Jesus is missing. His community is travelling back from their Passover celebrations in Jerusalem and Jesus is not present with them. Luke describes Jesus' parents taking primary concern for his upbringing and journeying back to find him. They eventually track him down in the temple courts sitting amongst the religious teachers, listening to them and asking questions. Here we see the religious community (the teachers in the temple), the wider community (in whose company it was presumed Jesus had been travelling) and his inner family, all encircling Jesus. These places of influence are not so dissimilar to the *Growing Faith* nexus that Wolfe set out with church (temple?), school (wider community?) and household (inner family?) gathered around the child or young person, together seeking their spiritual growth and flourishing.

Today the situation is far from the model set out in the Bible since most under 18s are being raised in households where not only are their parents no longer actively identifying as Christians, but increasingly neither are their grandparents. Even for those being raised in Christian homes, research suggests that only 33% of adults prioritize the discipleship of their children.[8] Support needs to be given to both the family and the young person by both school and church working thoughtfully in committed partnership.

The *Growing Faith Foundation* was set up to support a culture shift from one where households, schools and churches were working relatively independently towards a context in which there is an intentionality of partnership between the three, with the child positioned at the centre.

How Often Do Our Circles Operate in Isolation and What Culture Shift is Needed?

The Church Pastoral Aid Society (CPAS), an Anglican Mission agency, works across the country to support the delivery of 'School Ventures'—residentials for churches and schools to participate in together, giving pupils space to unpack *The Case of the Empty Tomb* (an RE teaching resource accredited by *Understanding Christianity* that enables pupils to look in depth at the crucifixion and resurrection narratives and ask questions of them).

Following one such residential, a volunteer leader was saddened to realize that the opportunities for the children from his locality to continue their investigation into Christianity were limited. He worked with the school to set up a group in which pupils could explore their big spiritual questions. It met in school, led by church members. Pupils came and brought their friends. In many ways this seemed like success.

But the years since have told a different story. Without buy-in and culture shift in the local church, these children were never able to step beyond school as their place of spiritual journeying. The church services were not approached in ways that made them accessible to these question-asking youngsters or their families. Although the children briefly attended, they were unable to settle and find welcome. When the children transitioned from primary to secondary, contact with them was lost.

How is the *Growing Faith Foundation* setting about leading this culture shift? Through investing in four workstreams:

- *Developing leaders:* through the Growing Faith Strategic Leaders Programme, which draws together paid and unpaid leaders from schools, churches, diocesan staff and parachurch organizations to learn from one another, developing their leadership competencies and confidence so as to bring sustainable change for children and young people.
- *Research:* both commissioning some and disseminating more.
- *Networks and learning hubs:* hubs offer opportunity for experimentation and the networks are spaces for connection, support, peer learning, updates and reflection.
- *Listening to the voices of children and young people* and amplifying these.

The approach of the *Growing Faith Foundation* is intentionally very un-prescriptive in terms of actions, but very focused instead on learning together and relationship. It tries to keep the voices of children and young people central and works hard to be as diverse a community as possible.

So Why is All This Good News—What Are the Opportunities?

From a School Perspective

- Churches are being actively encouraged to work in closer partnership with their local school(s) and to have a better understanding of the Church of England's *Vision for Education.*
- Clergy training is being adjusted to highlight the importance of partnership with schools and to provide the necessary knowledge and skills to support this.

- Clergy appointments are being approached with a greater appreciation of parish context, looking to incorporate the local school(s) more where possible.
- The availability of chaplaincy (lay and ordained) is increasing, with pathways of support and training for this being developed.
- Schools are being made better aware of supporting resources/ organizations.
- The central Church of England is looking to support the training and recruitment of 3000 additional employed children's and youth workers, who will be encouraged to serve their local pupils and families. This is in addition to thousands of unpaid lay leaders.
- Money has been made available through diocesan education teams for the *FLOURISH* network (establishing worshipping communities in schools and colleges).
- All of the above support many of the SIAMS requirements.

From a Church Perspective

- The support available to churches in order to work effectively with their local school is growing. This includes:
  - ◊ Better training for lay and ordained leaders
  - ◊ Clearer signposting to resources available
  - ◊ Grants for partnership work
  - ◊ Opportunities for mutual strategic planning by clergy and head teachers
  - ◊ Increased provision for the recruitment, training and continuing development of children's and youth workers (both paid and volunteer)
- The 2019 and 2023 updates of the SIAMS schedule laid greater emphasis on the partnership between school and church, meaning that church schools more actively welcome support from their local church(es).
- The requirement for church schools to have a vision statement, that is theologically underpinned and which informs all aspects of school life, forms a strong basis for the school-church partnership.

From a Household Perspective

There is recognition that increasingly few households are equipped to support the spiritual development of their young people and that, even in Christian households, for many this is not a key priority.[9] Consequently, there is now increasing assistance being offered in this area. For example:

- Churches are running courses like *Parenting for Faith*, offering intentional discipleship of parents to encourage them, and signposting other resources available.[10]
- Schools are facilitating spiritual development via content in school newsletters, through activities sent home *eg* Bible passages to read for homework, or activities like building Easter gardens or a prayer space, and by more clearly signposting how the church can help.

Churches are growing their prioritization of children and young people. This is leading to services that increasingly have their needs in mind, often in an intergenerational context. Many churches are also creating additional discipleship opportunities for children and young people and their families.

Questions to Consider

- The biblical model places the emphasis on the family as the primary place of spiritual development for children, with support from the wider community (church and school). What would it look like for school and church to collaborate well, to support families with this?
- What excites and encourages you about *Growing Faith*? Does anything discourage or frustrate you?

Collaboration

4

In the last chapter, we examined *Growing Faith* as the nexus of household, school and church working together with the spiritual development and flourishing of children and young people and their families at the centre. For the remainder of this book, we will focus in upon the school's role within this nexus.

At interview, prospective church school head teachers are likely to be asked how they will lead the school community, both pupils and adults, to enable the spiritual development and flourishing of all. At appointment, clergy are given responsibility for the spiritual health of their parish, which includes the school community. How then do these two key leaders i) understand and ii) work out these overlapping responsibilities? Do they hold a shared understanding of the nature and goal of any partnership? Does it matter if they do not?

An unpublished CPAS study of head teachers asked them to 'list five ways in which you would like the support of your local church.' The strongest theme that came out was *relationship*. Head teachers wanted:

- Opportunity to plan together for the spiritual development of pupils.
- Support with their own personal spiritual journey, and how to lead others in prayer and worship where they may not be confident of this themselves.
- Help with pastoral support for pupils, staff and families.
- Shared projects that would link the school and church communities more obviously. Examples given included craft projects that would centre on the pupils; opportunities to come together in shared worship; prayer spaces in school; joint school and church coffee mornings in which they support parents together; sharing resources to assist vulnerable families.

In a report recently commissioned by the *Growing Faith Foundation* into the hallmarks of effective church-school partnerships where pupils' spiritual development is best supported, the first listed headline finding was:

> The greater the involvement from the church in the school, both in terms of the number of people involved and in terms of frequency of contact, the greater the contribution to the spiritual development of the children.[11]

Again, this highlights the importance of relationship. This report found that the relationship between the head teacher and clergy person was of great significance, but also that the intentional broadening of this relationship, so that it was cherished between the wider school and church communities, was vital.

The CPAS study of head teachers cited above, all of whom considered themselves to have a strong partnership with their local church (which was validated in their most recent SIAMS report), uncovered that there were many, varied factors that challenged the effective functioning of their partnership:

- Perception by one or both leaders that the other was busy, leaving them reticent to explore the potential for deeper collaboration.
- Past negative experiences of other church-school partnerships.
- Challenges of geography such as the partner church(es) not being easily walkable from the school.
- Dwindling or aging congregation at the church making broader connections harder.
- The DBS and safer recruitment requirements presenting a barrier to volunteers.
- Lack of clarity on how purpose/vision could be shared.

So, if partnership is so dependent upon relationships between the head teacher and clergy person, together with wider school and church community, how can we work towards deeper, more effective collaboration?

Reflecting on partnerships, Sir David Carter (Former National Schools Commissioner Feb 2016-Aug 2018) noted that 'successful collaboration needs a purpose.' During a presentation in 2023 at the Guildford Diocesan Education Conference, he observed five tests that can indicate how healthy a collaboration is:

- *Purpose:* Does everyone involved know and share the intended outcome?
- *Mutuality:* Does the collaboration enable all partners to grow and flourish or is the benefit flowing in only one direction?

- *Change:* What are you hoping to change by entering the partnership—and is this happening (or is the situation stagnant)?
- *Pace:* Is there a timescale to review the effectiveness of the collaboration?
- *Prioritization:* It is going to cost everyone—what will you stop to enable this collaboration to be the priority?

Each of these tests offers a helpful way for school SLT (senior leadership team) and church leaders to reflect on purposeful collaboration.

Purpose

There is a need for school and church leaders to have an honest conversation not only about where their areas of commonality lie but also where there is a difference of focus and potential for conflict. As noted in the introduction, many Christians, if asked, take seriously the Great Commission of Matthew 28 to make disciples of all nations. They long in their hearts to see others join them in God's family. The extent to which they seek to evangelize may vary hugely, but their heart is to see God's kingdom grow. They do so aware of the difficulties of sharing faith in a pluralist world, in which secularism and post-modernism increase the complexity of the task.

Church schools are committed to offering an education for the whole community—and in many areas there are no other options available to parents. The school therefore needs to be a safe place of welcome for families who may not consider themselves Christian, or indeed who may hold another committed faith or worldview of their own and not want this to be undermined. Sometimes, where leaders have failed to acknowledge these differences, there has been relational difficulty that has marred effective partnership. Where differences are acknowledged and respected, then there is ground for healthy, trusting partnership.

Growing Faith suggests that the child or young person is placed at the centre of the purpose. Thus, a shared aim of the school and the church, around which collaboration can happen, is not to create a great relationship between school and church. That will be the by-product. Rather, it is to create an environment for nurturing the spiritual development of the child or young person, and to recognize that this will be enhanced where households are better enabled to support the process. School and church both have a role to play, sometimes separately, sometimes together. The key question then becomes: *What are the pathways to enabling a child or young person to grow spiritually, and who is best placed at each moment to support this?*

For some, the language of spiritual development is problematic. Some schools struggled when the language of SIAMS pivoted away from 'distinctively Christian' and underscored the school's role in pupils' spiritual development. A diocesan adviser told me of one church school's response, which was to seek help from organizations with spiritualities beyond the church. Why? Because they did not know what spiritual development was and did not think that this was something connected with Christianity. That school was not alone in their thinking, and their response helps us to understand why the language of spiritual development can be unhelpful for some. Happily, the diocesan education team in question were able to respond and support all their schools with uncovering a deeper understanding of i) spiritual development and ii) specifically *Christian* spiritual development.

What then is a pupil's Christian spiritual development, around which the *Growing Faith* adventure orbits? There are many definitions on offer. One that might work well is: 'The search for God, in response to God's search for us.'[12] Christians in ages past have worked out their spiritual development through a range of spiritual practices (also known as Christian disciplines), centring themselves on the person and teachings of Jesus as revealed in the Bible. At different points in church history, or in diverse expressions of churchmanship, various practices have come to the fore.

For many of these practices, such as sung worship or prayer, there are multiple, varied expressions of the same fundamental practice. For example, sung worship might be experienced through Benedictine chant, organ-led choral music or band-led singing; prayer could be undertaken as led liturgical prayer, spontaneous corporate prayer or personal prayer-space activities. In my experience, pupils report finding it helpful to be given opportunities to explore the Christian disciplines in a range of forms.

It is worth noting that other religions use their own forms of some of these spiritual practices. For example, consider the ubiquity of prayer. This means that thought needs to be given as to the specifically *Christian* version of these spiritual practices. Below is a list of common Christian disciplines which the school and church may wish to consider exploring with pupils. It omits some disciplines, such as fasting, that are not necessarily helpful in many school-led contexts, and which might be better left to the church to explore with their congregation:

- Prayer
- Bible reading
- Sung worship
- Sharing holy communion
- Giving

- Service of others
- Pilgrimage or retreat
- Confession
- Silence and solitude
- Fellowship with others

Mutuality

Who is the mutuality between? If the desire for collaboration between schools, churches and households is for the sake of pupils' spiritual development, surely this would make the mutuality between the triumvirate of school, church and home? But perhaps this runs the risk of encouraging the church to see collaboration as merely a means to an end, whereby they might reverse their declining Sunday attendance. Perhaps seeing the mutuality as being between pupils and a combination of other partners (school, church and household being the main contenders) is more helpful, as this keeps the young person more firmly at the centre?

In many situations, children and young people lack agency, yet studies show that where their voice and their contribution is valued, where they can ask questions and seek understanding, where they can bring leadership, this becomes a place of spiritual growth and blessing to the wider school and church communities. As noted in chapter two, when the new head teacher arrived at my school and gave agency to the pupils, this became both transformational for my class and also hugely enriching for me and for other adults within the school.

I saw this principle exemplified well recently at a school where a self-selecting group of Year 6 children were supported to create a series of prayer spaces to accompany their leavers' service. The children worked with a Christian teaching assistant to design, resource and set up prayer activities in the graveyard outside the church. Parents, carers and wider family were encouraged to arrive 45 minutes early for the service so that they could participate *with* their children in the prayer stations, each one being hosted by the Year 6 prayer leaders. Activities included washing mud off stones (confession), blowing bubbles (to release anxieties to God) and cutting out a hand shape (using it to pray for family members).

The head teacher's reflection on the morning was that the whole community had participated—those of Christian faith, those of other faiths and those of none. Everyone came and engaged. She was fascinated that it was one of the few occasions in which pupils engaged spiritually alongside their key adults and younger siblings, rather than in isolation at school away from families. It caused her to ponder whether there were other ways to further support this type of household experience throughout the year.

She noted that somehow it was easier for the community to be drawn in because of the fact it had been led by the children. Other adult-led prayer activities at the school had not been as universally or deeply engaged with.

The rector noted that the engagement with the church service afterwards had been deeper and more open than in previous years. In the prayer spaces beforehand there had been tears and laughter. People told stories of profound moments of encounter, able to pray about things that they had previously kept hidden. This left them ready for engagement with the more formal church service.

Change

Partnerships exist for a variety of reasons. Where they have formed to bring change, it is startling how often things can stagnate. Collaborative activities can often be continued for years without critique. How can you ensure that your partnership(s) have inbuilt opportunities for robust review, thereby ensuring that they can continue to meet expectations? One common problem is loss of focus. What started out as a clear goal to deepen opportunities for pupils' spiritual development subtly morphs into the aim of fostering a closer partnership between church and school, whilst the pupils' spiritual journey ends up no longer central.

A school and church had a shared desire to give pupils an opportunity to explore Christian worship more deeply than was possible through school singing practice. They particularly wanted to make this opportunity accessible for the vast majority of pupils who did not attend church. The vision was to launch a week-night 'choir church,' led by the church, meeting as an after-school club but on church premises so that the children became familiar with the church building and local Christians. They wanted the choir church to act as a bridge for pupils between school community and church community.

Choir church did not go as planned. Struggling to find anyone from the church community to lead the singing and explore worship more deeply, they employed a non-Christian music teacher to the role. Complexity with risk assessments and safeguarding required a change of location from church to school. Those who engaged were mostly the few children who already regularly attended church, rather than those who were less familiar with it.

Fascinatingly, the church and school leaders reflected eagerly that it was a great success because their personal relationship had deepened from running it, because the children enjoyed it and because the church family appreciated the children occasionally *performing* in church. No reference was made regarding the spiritual impact on the children or on whether it lived up to any of the vision that had birthed it, in particular to make exploring worship accessible for those not already participating in Christian community.

Pace

Across multiple dioceses, with schools and churches of different traditions, there is one activity that, if prioritized, has had more impact than anything else: diary time. Where school and church leaders prioritize meeting, significant change almost always occurs. Leaders who consider their purpose together across a range of time frames and set careful short, medium and long-term targets see the most impact.

- *Big picture:* Where are you hoping to be in five years?
- *Middle distance:* What are your goals for the year ahead?
- *Small scale:* How are the stepping stones to the above working; does anything need changing?

Big picture: Some partnerships work well by having an annual meeting with multiple stakeholders, *eg* a slot at a governing body meeting to which key church/PCC members are invited. They consider carefully how to include pupil voices and household perspectives within this, as they discuss the big picture.

Middle distance: eg a termly meeting with the key leaders such as: the head teacher, RE lead, a Christian staff member, clergy person, lay volunteer, key Christian parent and pupil leaders. They discuss the middle distance, review the term and set goals for the next term.

Small scale: Usually conducted informally *eg* five minutes pencilled in after Collective Worship or via emails, messages and conversations at the school gates.

Prioritization

One of the challenging questions that Sir David Carter regularly asks is: 'What do you have to give up in order for a partnership to succeed?' He notes that:

> Effective and meaningful collaboration does not come without its challenges. From my experience, it is not unusual to find that many school leaders and governing bodies believe that autonomy from any form of external influence or direction is sacrosanct, and as a result they can become disinterested observers and passive participants in collaboration. This is a tendency we must overcome if we are to succeed together.[13]

Churches can often be similar.

Both schools and churches are busy, with both suffering with particular post-pandemic pressures, a nationally recognized lack of volunteers and with the current economic downturn. They have more to do, yet far fewer resources and volunteers with which to do it. Given this, Sir David Carter's question above holds more value (and more challenge!).

Collaboration is worthwhile but takes investment and a willingness to go at a shared pace. Partnership is desired by most but takes commitment. Hopefully the reflections above on purpose, mutuality, change, pace and prioritization will enable some good conversations between you and your other local collaborators.

Questions to Consider

- Near the start of the chapter, the CPAS head teacher study highlighted various factors that made partnership more difficult. Which resonated most with you?
- How can you make use of Sir David Carter's five measures of effective partnership (purpose, mutuality, change, pace and prioritization) to assess your current partnerships?
- How can you keep this all firmly centred on your pupils and their families and avoid slipping into the primary focus being the school-church partnership?

Pupil-focused

5

The *Faith in the Nexus* research indicated that children and young people are 'often the dynamic initiators of conversations about faith or spirituality' but that 'responding to children's talk about faith is challenging; adults may struggle with how to respond, avoid, or close down such conversations.'[14] It concludes that:

> Schools, families and the church needs to restore their faith in the Nexus [the creative interworking of these three institutions] and the possibility of what that interplay could bring...There is a clear need...to focus on children's spiritual well-being and recognize that making opportunities for children's faith exploration in the home must be a priority.[15]

The report recommends that, in most contexts, parents need the support of both school and church around them in order not to be 'discouraged by uncertainty, or lack of confidence in knowing what to say.'

As children and young people explore their questions and worldview, they need:

- Space, time and encouragement to consider their own thinking and assumptions
- Relationships where questioning and exploration are welcomed
- Core Christian teaching to be carefully explained
- Opportunity to glimpse something of the inner life of others to inform their own journey

For many years, the seminal work on children's spiritual development has been Rebecca Nye's *Children's Spirituality: What it is and Why it Matters*. In it, she looks at the conditions which foster its growth, using an acrostic to present her thinking:

S: Space
P: Process
I: Imagination
R: Relationship
I: Intimacy
T: Trust

Space

This references both the physical space as well as the emotional and auditory space. Children are sensitive to the feel of a space. If you are leading Collective Worship in school, consider how you might shape the space:

- How will the pupils come in and go out: will music play or will you use silence? How will people move and arrange themselves in the space?
- What does the tidiness / clutteredness of the space communicate?
- Are there symbols and / or rituals you can use as a bridge to the sacred: lighting a candle; using a special table at the front, maybe with an artefact like a cross or with a worship cloth; repeated liturgy like 'Peace be with you / And also with you'; perhaps drawing a curtain across untidy areas to create a different feel?

You may also want to consider how you can support pupils to develop other spaces in their lives. This support might collaborate with households to enable development of deeply personal and intimate spaces like a prayer corner / table / ritual in their bedroom, or a garden den. Or more corporately, facilitating communal spaces such as a prayer space in the school or church grounds, or prayer around a family meal. One aspect of space that is lacking from children's lives is *time*. Many children lead lives that are incredibly busy and report that without moments of stillness and quiet, that they find it hard to engage spiritually.

Process

Nye writes: 'Spirituality is more about process than product…Production suggests that the end result is important…Prayer and worship are spiritual processes, not ends in themselves.'[16] Often when pupils do contribute to leading in services at school or church, their contribution might be described as 'product.' What would it take to change this?

Imagination

Notice how often Jesus used parables or analogies to explain spiritual matters. Children come alive when presented with opportunity to seek meaning themselves. This was modelled by the head teacher mentioned in chapter two. Drama, art, music, literature and play can all unlock deeper spirituality.

Relationship

Rachel Turner, founder of *Parenting for Faith*, writes that:

> God has wired our brains…to learn by watching and trying things. Developing a relationship with God is no different. When parents give their children glimpses of their relationship with God in the everyday bits of life, it's like creating a window for them to see a real two-way connection with him.[17]

Head teachers are often keen to facilitate different local Christians coming into school to show what their faith journey looks like and to answer pupil questions. They want their pupils to glimpse the diversity of how different Christians journey in relationship with God, in order to inform pupils' own spiritual development.

Intimacy

We can experience intimacy with God in different ways. It does not have to be about seeking private spaces. Consider times when you have brought pupils to church and they have fallen silent with a sense of reverence; or when you have looked together with awe at a landscape, seascape, sunset or the stars. Often people describe these as 'thin places' where God feels close. How might the school environment (prayer spaces?), trips and residentials play a part in helping pupils to find places where they feel safe, and surrender feels more natural?

Trust

Three questions that Nye poses for us to ponder:

- Is there room for greater trust *in God* in this process?
- Is there room for greater trust *in the child* in your approach?
- Is this approach signalling basic trust *in the faith* (the Bible, the liturgy, Christian doctrines)?

One critique of Nye is that sometimes the discussion of spirituality can feel a bit nebulous. This can happen when we divorce it from context. The soil for children's spiritual development in a church school and a church working in collaboration with households, is a growing understanding of the teachings of the Christian faith. A deepening appreciation for the big narrative of the Bible is the context. This was very helpfully set out in the *Understanding Christianity* RE resource with its frieze that engages thought around the journey of:[18]

- Creation
- The fall (rebellion from God, the breaking of relationship and explanation for why the world around us is broken)
- The people of God (Old Testament narrative of the Jewish people trying to live with God at the centre)
- Incarnation (birth of Jesus, God's Son)
- Gospel (Jesus' life, ministry, teaching)
- Salvation (impact of Jesus' death and resurrection)
- Kingdom of God (restoration)

An understanding of this, the big meta-narrative of the Bible, enables pupils to place the stories and teachings they hear within this framework, much as a pupil learning the history of the Victorians might learn where this fits into the bigger timeline of history. For teachers wishing to understand this more deeply, *The Bible Course* has now been made available in an adapted form for teachers to undertake together.[19]

As we collaborate between home, school and church so that pupils have opportunities for…

- Space, time and encouragement to consider their own thinking and assumptions
- Relationships where questioning and exploration are welcomed
- Core Christian teaching to be carefully explained
- Opportunity to glimpse something of the inner life of others to inform their own journey

…the following questions might help to shape our thinking:

- How are pupils being given space, time and encouragement to explore their own thinking—both at home and throughout the curriculum at school?
- Do your pupils have other ideas of what support they might like with their spiritual development—have you asked them?
- Are there ways to give room to pupils' reflections, questions and contributions within the pattern of Collective Worship? Which adults from both school and church(es) might support with this?
- How can you plan pathways for those who want to journey deeper, with multiple entry points and multiple places of deeper exploration? What is the role of your local church(es) in this?
- Do you facilitate pupils having access to a wider intergenerational Christian community or does it revolve around support from a single individual / small group? How can the former be enabled?
- In what ways are you empowering—or disempowering—the church community?
- How can households be best supported for their role of spiritual nurture—what can both school and church contribute to this?
- What might governors or MAT trustees be able to contribute to any planning or collaboration?

Questions to Consider

- How can you make use of Nye's SPIRIT observations to analyze your current approach?
- Which of the above questions is most pertinent to you as you plan your next steps? Who might join you to share their insights?

6 Final Reflection

Throughout writing this book, I have found myself drawn time and again to exploring the school-church dynamic rather than keeping the emphasis on the pupil remaining central to the whole discussion. It has taken the help of critical friends and much rewriting and editing to stay focused. I wonder whether you sense the same pull and how it impacts things in your context?

I remember, as a secondary pupil, encountering this Chinese proverb in class: 'I listen and I forget, I see and I remember, I do and I understand.' It struck me deeply at the time and later would become foundational to my teaching approach. So often, as adults, we treat children and young people as empty vessels to be filled, expecting them to listen, engage and remember. So often, we plan on their behalf but fail to give them sufficient agency to truly 'do and…understand.' I see this in classrooms; I see this in churches; I see this in households. Sometimes we present our children and young people with good visuals and stories to aid their learning, and undoubtedly this helps. At our best, sometimes we give them thoughtfully-chosen practical activities that embed the learning more deeply and expose places where understanding is lacking. But what happens when we give them greater agency? What happens when we ask truly open questions? What happens when we let them lead and teach us and position ourselves as learners? What happens when we let them take risks and try things out for themselves?

Some of the most transformative contexts I have encountered have been where children and young people have been given agency. In this book, we saw this in:

- Chapter two: where my head teacher provided a rich diet of input, but the pupils were given space to ponder, ask questions and respond, with their ideas being valued and amplified in the end of week Collective Worship.
- Chapter four: where the Year 6 pupils were given space to prepare and lead prayer activities before their leavers' service and the engagement of all was enabled.

These are merely two examples, though I know of many others that could be added from other school, church and household contexts around the country.

How did Jesus model spiritual development to us? He walked with his disciples. He used the encounters on the road, the messiness of life and the meals that they shared together as his moments for learning. He sent them out in pairs to go and try out his way. He gave them agency. When faced with a hungry crowd he initially left his disciples to work out for themselves how to feed them, letting them learn and understand by trying to 'do' (Mark 6.30–44). He fell asleep in a boat upon stormy waves, leaving his disciples to figure out what to do next. This would lead to a profound moment of understanding for them as they fearfully asked, 'Who is this? Even the wind and the waves obey him!' (Mark 4.35–41).

A challenge for us in twenty-first century Britain is that so few children have opportunity to 'do and...understand' in their homes because so few are situated in families that can journey any of this with them. The 'Faith in the Nexus' report, referenced in chapter five, highlighted this deficit. *Growing Faith* seeks to encourage us to find ways in which this deficiency can be overcome through the thoughtful support of pupils and households by schools and churches. Some of the complexities of this have been explored, not least the need for schools to be places where Christianity is presented invitationally, rather than confessionally, so that all children of all faiths and none can be 'present with integrity.'[20] Hopefully some of the reflections, questions and stories of this book will help you as you work out, in your context, what your next steps might look like.

Questions to Consider

- Can you pin down two next steps that you would like to take in response to this booklet? Who can you message to hold you accountable to this?
- With whom you could share this book so as to support greater collaboration?
- What questions do you need to ask the children and young people in your community so that they can remain at the centre of your next steps?

Notes

1 Attributed to Lord Runcie as quoted in *The Way Ahead* (London: Church House Publishing, 2012) p 4.

2 Well argued in T Cooling, *Doing God in Education* (London: Theos, 2010).

3 *Church of England Vision for Education: Deeply Christian, Serving the Common* (London: The Church of England Education Office, 2016) p 13.

4 *Growing Faith Paper GS2121,* found at https://www.cefel.org.uk/faithfulness/ (accessed June 2024).

5 https://www.churchofengland.org/about/education-and-schools/growing-faith-foundation/ (accessed June 2024).

6 See Appendix for some further thoughts for those embarking on this.

7 'Introduction to *Growing Faith'* found at https://www.cefel.org.uk/faithfulness/ (accessed June 2024).

8 https://www.theosthinktank.co.uk/research/2016/10/31/passing-on-faith/ (accessed June 2024). https://www.pewresearch.org/social-trends/2023/01/24/parenting-in-america-today/ (accessed June 2024).

9 https://nicer.org.uk/faith-in-the-nexus/ (accessed June 2024). See also links in note 8 above.

10 www.parentingforfaith.brf.org.uk/ (accessed June 2024).

11 https://www.churchofengland.org/sites/default/files/2023-10/guildford-diocese-growing-faith-research-report.pdf/ (accessed June 2024).

12 Jo Anne Taylor, quoted in R Nye, *Children's Spirituality: What it is and Why it Matters* (London: Church House Publishing, 2009), p 2.

13 https://qaeducation.co.uk/features/sir-david-carter/ (accessed June 2024).

14 https://nicer.org.uk/faith-in-the-nexus p 11 for both quotations (accessed June 2024).

15 *ibid,* p 88.

16 R Nye, *Children's Spirituality: What it is and Why it Matters* (London: Church House Publishing, 2009) p 46.

17 www.parentingforfaith.brf.org.uk/ (accessed June 2024).

18 https://www.understandingchristianity.org.uk/ (accessed June 2024).

19 https://www.biblesociety.org.uk/explore-the-bible/the-bible-course/the-bible-course-for-teachers/ (accessed June 2024).

20 *Statutory Inspection of Anglican and Methodist Schools—An Evaluation Schedule for Schools and Inspectors* (London: The Church of England Education Office, revised 2021). Available online at: https://www.churchofengland.org/sites/default/files/2021-09/siams-revised-evaluation-schedule-september-2021-annotated-version.pdf (accessed June 2024) p 19.